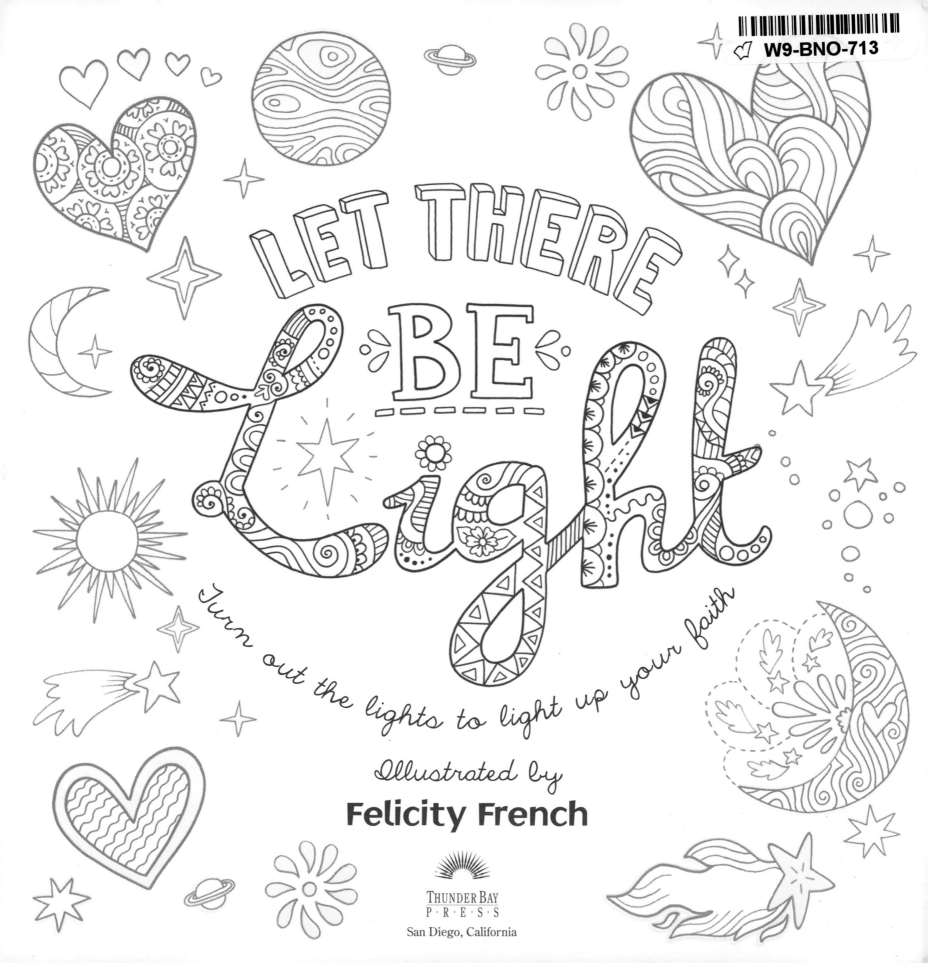

LET THERE BE Light

Turn out the lights to light up your faith

Illustrated by

Felicity French

THUNDER BAY
P·R·E·S·S

San Diego, California

W9-BNO-713

Color your way closer to God

We live in such a busy, hectic world, but this book offers you an opportunity to spend some time with God.

Before you start

Try to spend a few minutes in prayer or reading the Bible before you select a verse to color. This will ensure that when your mind starts wandering, your focus is on Godly thoughts.

It doesn't matter which page you select to color, but it is essential to center your mind on the verse. If you can't focus on the whole verse, pick one word or one idea, and ask God what it is he wants you to hear. Open yourself up to God's guidance.

A form of prayer

Recite the verse as you color the patterns and pictures, and reflect on its relevance to you. This is a form of prayer. Be aware of God's presence as you color and meditate on the words. God is always with you, but it is likely that you often forget that throughout your day. This is a time to embrace that closeness with the Lord. It will help you to gradually become aware of God's presence over the whole day, not just during moments of prayer and focus.

As you color the art and are absorbed in it, you can meditate on God's words. The colors will help you to relax, and give you pleasure. Remember, it is the process that counts. It doesn't matter if you end up with a masterpiece or a page full of scribbles. There should be no pressure to create something that needs approval of others. It is the quality of the time between you and God that matters.

Mount and glow

When you've finished coloring each verse, mount it on your wall to remind you of God's words. The pages are easy to remove along the perforated inside edge of each page.

Some pages are coated in glow ink—you will spot the sheen. When these special pages have been under a light source for at least thirty seconds, the selected pictures and words will glow in the dark. Let them light up your faith.

Prayers and devotions

The last section of the book (pages 85 to 95) invites you to write your own prayers and devotions. By praying every day, you will develop a stronger relationship with God.

the Word
GAVE LIFE TO
EVERYTHING
that was created,
AND HIS LIFE
brought light to
EVERYONE.
John 1:4

LET EVERYTHING that has breath PRAISE the Lord.

Psalm 150:6

The heavens declare the glory of God, and the sky above proclaims his handiwork.

Psalm 19:1

We love each other because **he** loved us first.

1 John 4:19

HE
counts
the
stars
and calls them
all by name.

PSALM 147:4

Rejoice
in the
Lord
always.

PHILIPPIANS 4:4

THINK *about the* THINGS OF HEAVEN, *not the things of earth.*

COLOSSIANS 3:2

Taste and see that the Lord is good!

Psalm 34:8

When you pass through the waters, I will be with you.

Isaiah 43:2

Those who **trust** in the **Lord** will find new **strength**. They will soar high on wings like eagles.

Isaiah 40:31

With
GOD
all
THINGS
are
possible.

Mark 10:27

FOR he WILL ORDER HIS angels TO protect YOU WHEREVER YOU GO.

PSALM 91:11

I can do all things through **Christ,** who *strengthens* me.

Philippians 4:13

As a deer longs for streams of water,

SO I LONG FOR YOU, GOD.

Psalm 42:1

I said,
"I am falling";
but
*your constant
love, O Lord,*
held me up.

PSALM 94:18

Your word is a lamp to guide my feet and a LIGHT FOR MY PATH.

PSALM 119:105

In the beginning was the **Word**, and the **Word** was with **GOD**,

and the **Word** was **GOD.**

John 1:1

Come to me, all you who are weary and burdened, and I will give you rest.

MATTHEW 11:28

Children are a gift from the Lord.

Psalm 127:3

GIVE THANKS TO THE **LORD**, for he is good. His love endures forever.

Psalm 136:1

JESUS CHRIST

is the same

yesterday and today

and

FOREVER.

HEBREWS 13:8

I am the good shepherd.

John 10:11

The Lord is gracious and compassionate, slow to anger and rich in love.

PSALM 145:8-10

Blessed is the one who trusts in the Lord.

PROVERBS 16:20

In the beginning God created the heavens and the earth.

GENESIS 1:1

The Lord is my
LIGHT
and my
SALVATION.

Psalm 27:1

Do to others as you would have them do to you.

LUKE 6:31

You are the light of the world.

MATTHEW 5:14

A friend LOVES at all times.

PROVERBS 17:17

The name of the
Lord is a
fortified tower;
the righteous
run to it and are
safe.

PROVERBS 18:10

Delight yourself in the *Lord*, and *he will give you* the *desires* of your *heart.*

PSALM 37:4

Hatred stirs up conflict, but **love covers over all wrongs.**

Proverbs 10:12

The Lord loves righteousness and justice; the earth is full of his unfailing love.

PSALM 33:5

Search me, O God, and know my heart.

PSALM 139:23

Who teaches us more than the beasts of the earth, And makes us wiser than the birds of heaven?

Job 35:11

The Lord your God is with you wherever you go.

Joshua 1:9

I keep my eyes always on the Lord. With him at my right hand, I will not be shaken.

Psalm 16:8

Let all that YOU DO be done IN LOVE.

1 Corinthians 16:14

This is the day
THE LORD HAS MADE;
We will rejoice
and be glad
in it.

Psalm 118:24

PRAYERS AND DEVOTIONS

PRAYERS AND DEVOTIONS

PRAYERS AND DEVOTIONS

PRAYERS AND DEVOTIONS

PRAYERS AND DEVOTIONS

PRAYERS AND DEVOTIONS

PRAYERS AND DEVOTIONS

PRAYERS AND DEVOTIONS

PRAYERS AND DEVOTIONS

PRAYERS AND DEVOTIONS

PRAYERS AND DEVOTIONS

Thunder Bay Press
An imprint of Printers Row Publishing Group
10350 Barnes Canyon Road, Suite 100
San Diego, CA 92121
www.thunderbaybooks.com

Printers Row Publishing Group is a division of Readerlink Distribution Services, LLC. Thunder Bay Press is a registered trademark of Readerlink Distribution Services, LLC.

All notations of errors or omissions should be addressed to Thunder Bay Press, Editorial Department, at the above address. All other correspondence (author inquiries, permissions) concerning the content of this book should be addressed to Red Bird Publishing Ltd., U.K. www.red-bird.co.uk

Thunder Bay Press
Publisher: Peter Norton
Associate Publisher: Ana Parker
Publishing/Editorial Team: Kathryn C. Dalby, April Farr
Editorial Team: JoAnn Padgett, Melinda Allman, Dan Mansfield

ISBN: 978-1-68412-723-8
Printed in China
23 22 21 20 19   3 4 5 6 7

Illustrated by Felicity French
Written by Susan Hayes
Development, production & glow art:
Red Bird Publishing Ltd., U.K.
www.red-bird.co.uk